The Gems of Heaven

John B. Mulder

PublishAmerica
Baltimore

First printing

Grammatical review and editing of this manuscript was provided by Wilma D. Mulder, B.S., English and Literature, former high school teacher.

ISBN: 1-4241-4607-0
PUBLISHED BY PUBLISHAMERICA, LLLP
www.publishamerica.com
Baltimore

Printed in the United States of America

This book is dedicated to my mother, Maria Johanna. She immigrated to the United States from the Netherlands in 1914, settled in northwest Iowa, and later married another Dutch immigrant, Bastian Mulder. They had 11 children, one of whom died in infancy. Maria was a devout Christian who knew and greatly loved her Dutch Bible. She always had ready answers to any questions her children asked. Although never gaining earthly fame, she was a true gem to her family and friends. Because of her interest in all of God's creation, the author often asked her about the beauties of nature and heaven.

Table of Contents

Preface

Throughout the ages, heaven has been portrayed as man's highly desired final destination. Heaven, also called the Holy City and the New Jerusalem in scripture, is where all redeemed will spend eternity with God, Jesus, the angels, a great host of Old Testament saints, and New Testament believers. The actual beauty of heaven remains somewhat of a mystery. Much is still unknown about the Holy City; however, many glimpses of its grandeur are revealed in scripture. God, Himself, will provide unending divine illumination in the New Jerusalem. The magnificence of the gold, pearls, and multiple precious stones that will make up heaven will be enjoyed by God's children forever.

This book depicts what is known currently about the gems of heaven as their identity is revealed in scripture. During past history, information about the Holy City's gems was conveyed through multiple generations. However, the possibility exists that the materials seen by the apostle John could differ from what is known about today's gems with identical names. Should any descriptions in this book be inaccurate, be assured that the beauty of the New Jerusalem will certainly surpass the insights provided by any human author.

Gemstones are inorganic minerals that may be fashioned into various shapes. They are generally beautiful, rare, and durable. Pearls are organic gems that are produced by animals. Gold is a precious metal that is not a gemstone but is often included in this group.

In order to appreciate heaven's gems more fully, understanding their various properties is helpful. Parameters that will be evaluated include sources, composition, current uses, colors, hardness, specific gravity, refractive indexes, and double refraction values. Durability of gems is measured by using the Mohs scale of mineral hardness as developed by the German scientist, Friedrich Mohs in 1812. The hardness scale values, which are somewhat arbitrary, are as follows: 2.5 can be scratched by a fingernail, 2.5 to 3 represents the hardness of gold or silver, 3 a copper penny, 4 to 4.5 platinum, 4.5 iron, 5.5 a knife blade, 6 glass, 6.5 iron pyrite, and 7+ a hardened steel file. Specific gravity is measured by determining the weight of the amount of water that is replaced by the volume of a gem. This parameter, which is actually weight, is measured in grams per cubic centimeter.

The refractive index compares the relation between the speed of light in air to that in the gem. This index causes deviation or bending of light rays. These measurements are made by using a refractometer. The refractive index remains constant for each gem and is used for identification purposes. Several gems have double refraction values, thus causing two deviations in transmitted or reflected light rays. Color of gems depends upon the way they absorb light. White light consists of all colors of the rainbow; the colored rays not absorbed are reflected back causing a gem's color. Since values for the properties of gems vary slightly, as determined by different gemologists, average assessments or ranges are used in this book.

Several authors have detailed the massive size of heaven, along with its glorious mansions that await the redeemed. Likely, at this very hour, specific preparations are underway to ensure total joy and happiness for all those who will dwell in heaven throughout the endless years of eternity. Before delineating information about the specific gems of heaven, an overview of the Holy City will be provided initially, followed by details about the various structural elements of the New Jerusalem.

Chapter 1
Heaven: A Desired Destination

God's redeemed children are promised eternal life in a real created place called heaven. The first verse in the Bible announced the creation or preparation of heaven. "In the beginning God created the heavens and the earth" (Genesis 1:1). Those anticipating a heavenly home as their eventual destination must be prepared by accepting God's free gift of salvation. "In this the love of God was manifested toward us, that God has sent His only begotten Son into the world, that we might live through Him. In this is love, not that we loved God, but that He loved us and sent His Son to be the propitiation for our sins" (1 John 4:9-10). Although there are those who question the existence of an actual site named heaven, the Bible mentions this glorious place more than 600 times. Yes, heaven is indeed a wonderful and beautiful creation designed by Almighty God for His children.

Although numerous excellent Bible scholars have written and spoken about the various aspects of heaven and the home going of saints to this glorious destination, universal agreement does not prevail. The author of this chapter presents information he concluded as correct from detailed study about heaven and its inhabitants. However, should eventual citizens of the Holy City find any of these conclusions to be in error, it is certain that the actual events and conditions involving this eternal home will be indescribably wonderful and satisfying.

Heaven and earth, as known today, will be destroyed to set the stage for God's creation of a new heaven and new earth. "But the day of the Lord will come as a thief in the night, in which the heavens will pass away with a great noise, and the elements will melt with fervent heat: both the earth and the works that are in it will be burned up" (2 Peter 3:10). "Now I saw a new heaven and a new earth, for the first heaven and the first earth had passed away. Also there was no more sea" (Revelation 21:1). This new heaven is also called the New Jerusalem or Holy City. God will demolish the old earth and heaven by a massive and noisy judgmental fire. Out of this spoil, totally new entities will be formed.

The exact location of heaven is unknown. First, Second, and Third Heavens are revealed in scripture. The First Heaven is called the firmament or is also known as the atmosphere. "Then God said, let there be a firmament in the midst of the waters, and let it divide the waters from the waters. Thus God made the firmament, and divided the waters which were under the firmament from the waters which were above the firmament; and it was so" (Genesis 1:6-7). In this expanse, clouds form, rain and storms originate, and birds fly. Outer space above the atmosphere consists of the Second Heaven and the planets and stars are located in this area. "Then God made two great lights: the greater light to rule the day, and the lesser light to rule the night. He made the stars also. God set them in the firmament of the heavens to give light on the earth" (Genesis 1:16-17). God dwells in the Third Heaven. "The Lord is high above all nations, His glory above the heavens. Who is like the Lord our God, Who dwells on high" (Psalm 113:4-5). Currently, the location of this site has not been unveiled to man.

There are Bible scholars who believe that. during the future Millennial Kingdom, following the rapture, the heavenly city or New Jerusalem will be in existence as a satellite suspended above the earth. This belief has some credence since Christ and His glorified saints will rule the earth during this time. With heaven nearby, movement between the earth and heaven would be facilitated. The apostle John described the New Jerusalem as coming down out of heaven, supporting the premise that it may be a satellite city. "Then I, John, saw the holy city, New Jerusalem, coming down out of heaven from God, prepared as a bride adorned for her husband" (Revelation 21:2).

Many details about heaven are yet unknown. However, scripture does give several insights about those who will populate this magnificent destination. God is omnipresent but His dwelling place and throne are located in heaven. "The Lord has established His throne in heaven, And His kingdom rules over all" (Psalm 103:19). It is clear that God's center of administration and authority are located in heaven. Here is where He rules over all the universe, welcomes worship from His saints, and hears their prayers. While angels minister to all mankind on earth, they maintain their permanent homes in heaven. The writer of Hebrews substantiates this fact stating, "But you

10

have come to Mount Zion and to the city of the living God, the heavenly Jerusalem, to an innumerable company of angels" (Hebrews 12:22). Also inhabiting heaven are the cherubim and seraphim who attend the throne of God, giving praise and showing obedience to Him.

All those who accepted Christ as their Savior will be in heaven. The Old Testament saints, and all who died prior to the resurrection of Christ, left their abode in Sheol (The Bosom of Abraham), which was located in the center of the earth, and their souls entered heaven when Christ was raised from the dead after His crucifixion. In Acts 2:31-32, the apostle Luke writes about David looking ahead to the resurrection of Christ, not being abandoned in Hades. "He, foreseeing this, spoke concerning the resurrection of Christ, that His soul was not left in Hades, nor did His flesh see corruption. This Jesus God has raised up, of which we are all witnesses." The patriarch, Abraham, looked forward by faith to his eventual heavenly destination. "By faith he dwelt in the land of promise as in a foreign country, dwelling in tents with Isaac and Jacob, and the heirs with him of the same promise; for he waited for the city which had foundations, whose builder and maker is God" (Hebrews 11:9-10).

The souls of Christians dying after Christ's crucifixion and resurrection were, and continue to be, ushered into heaven immediately after death. "So we are always confident, knowing that while we are at home in the body we are absent from the Lord. For we walk by faith, not by sight. We are confident, yes, well pleased rather to be absent from the body and to be present with the Lord" (2 Corinthians 5:6-8). When physical death occurs, the soul is separated from the body. After the last breath is taken, the souls of Christians access heaven instantly while their earthly bodies are left behind. For the Christian, death is only a comma in the story of life.

When Christ returns to the earth at the rapture, bodies of the redeemed dead will be raised from their grave sites first and, thereafter, the living saints on earth will be resurrected, all to be taken directly to heaven. The word, rapture, is not found in the Bible but it means *to be caught up* or *to be snatched up*. These verses describe the rapture; "For the Lord Himself will descend from heaven with a shout, with the voice of an archangel, and with the trumpet of God. And the dead in Christ will rise first. Then we who are alive and remain shall be caught up together with them in the clouds to meet the Lord in the air. And thus we shall always be with the Lord" (1 Thessalonians

4:16-17). Christ will not set foot on the earth during the rapture but saints will be caught up with him in the air.

All who entered heaven prior to the rapture will have intermediate bodies. Although information about the type of bodies received is unknown, individuals will retain their thoughts, feelings, desires, and personalities. Thus, pleasurable activities and interactions with other saints will continue. All the saints who entered heaven during the rapture, as well as all who were already in heaven, will have their bodies raised and these earthly resurrected bodies will be renewed as they are united with their souls. At this time, the bodies of all God's children dwelling in heaven will change from perishable to imperishable, from natural to spiritual. "So also is the resurrection of the dead. The body is sown in corruption, it is raised in incorruption. It is sown in dishonor, it is raised in glory. It is sown in weakness, it is raised in power. It is sown a natural body, it is raised a spiritual body. There is a natural body and there is a spiritual body" (1 Corinthians 15:42-44).

Following the rapture, all believers in heaven will appear before the Judgement Seat of Christ. Here the lives of all saints will be evaluated by Christ for their faithfulness while living on earth. Each saint will receive rewards as deemed appropriate by the risen Savior. These judgements will not review the sins of God's children since they were covered and paid for by the shed blood of the Savior on the cross at the time of the crucifixion.

A seven-year period of tribulation will follow the rapture. The last three and a half years of the tribulation will be an extremely difficult time under the tyrannic dictatorship of a godless ruler called the Antichrist. During this time, some will accept Christ as their Savior; they will suffer severe persecution and will likely be killed for their beliefs. Those Christians who are martyred during the tribulation period will enter heaven immediately as stated by the Apostle John in Revelation 14:13. "Then I heard a voice from heaven saying to me, "Write: Blessed are the dead who die in the Lord from now on." "Yes, says the Spirit, that they may rest from their labors, and their works follow them." As John reveals in this verse, it will be a blessing for these victimized saints to be released from suffering to enter their eternal rest.

At the end of the time of tribulation, there will be a 1,000-year period, known as the millennium. Christ will direct his saints who will rule over the earth with perfect justice at this time. An angel will appear and Satan will be bound and thrown into the bottomless pit as stated in Revelation 20:2-3. "He laid hold of the dragon, that serpent of old, who is the Devil and Satan, and bound him for a thousand years; and he cast him into the bottomless pit, and shut him up, and set a seal on him, so that he should deceive the nations no more till the thousand years were finished. But after these things he must be released for a little while."

Many people will be born and live during this millennial period. Most of these new persons will likely accept Christ; however, there will still be some who reject Christ and his redemption. At the end of this 1,000 year reign, Satan will be released for a short time. "Now when the thousand years have expired, Satan will be released from his prison and will go out and deceive the nations which are in the four corners of the earth, Gog and Magog, to gather them together to battle, whose number is as the sand of the sea" (Revelation 20:7-8). Thereafter, Christ will return to earth and all the lost who lived over past ages, plus those who died rejecting Christ during the millennium, will be raised up and judged at the Great White Throne Judgement. Additionally, those lost individuals living at the end of the millennium will also be judged at this time.

The Judgement Seat of Christ, which occurs immediately after the rapture, should not be confused with the Great White Throne Judgement. This final judgement will take place following Christ's appearance at the end of the millennium. At the Great White Throne, sinners will be judged and condemned to spend eternity in hell while those living saints who were born and accepted Christ during the millennial period will be ushered into heaven.

The Apostle John describes the Great White Throne Judgement as follows: "Then I saw a great white throne and Him who sat on it, from whose face the earth and heaven fled away. And there was found no place for them. And I saw the dead, small and great, standing before God, and books were opened. And another book was opened, which is the Book of Life. And the dead were judged according to their works, by the things which were written in the books. The sea gave up the dead who were in it, and Death and Hades delivered up the dead who were in them. And they were judged, each one according to their works. Then Death and Hades were cast into the lake of fire. This is the second death. And anyone not found written in the Book of Life was cast into the lake of fire" (Revelation 20:11-15).

Knowledge about those who will inhabit the Holy City and their experiences in this wonderful destination are intriguing and enlightening. Nothing sad nor painful will be allowed in heaven. Past trials and problems will no longer be present. "And God will wipe away every tear from their eyes; there shall be no more death, nor sorrow, nor crying. There shall be no more pain, for the former things have passed away" (Revelation 21: 4). If there are tears, they will be demonstrations of joy. Tears will no longer be shed as a result of broken hearts, disappointments, disasters, accidents, and injustices. No more fatal diseases, deaths, or funerals will occur. Sorrow from evildoers, sickness, broken families, loved one's failures, and the consequences of sins will be unknown. Pain now present at accident sites, on battlefields, in emergency rooms, or in cancer wards will cease.

No lonely nights will be spent in heaven, in fact, there will be no night. "The city had no need of the sun or of the moon to shine on it, for the glory of God illuminated it. The Lamb is its light. And the nations of those who are saved shall walk in its light, and the kings of the earth bring their glory and honor into it. Its gates shall not be shut at all by day (there shall be no night there)" (Revelation 21:23-25). There will be no sun and moon but God will provide light from his majestic radiant glory.

There will be no curse in heaven. "And there shall be no more curse, but the throne of God and of the Lamb shall be in it, and His servants shall serve Him" (Revelation 22:3). When Adam and Eve were driven from the Garden of Eden, God cursed the earth. To produce crops and raise animals, man needed to toil endlessly to control weeds, prevent diseases, and eliminate insects or parasites. Further, floods, hail, and storms formerly frustrated the cultivation of plants and rearing of animals. None of these former earthly curses will be present in heaven.

God's children will spend eternity with Jesus. He told the dying thief on a cross at the crucifixion that he would be in paradise with Him that very day. "And Jesus said to him, Assuredly, I say to you, today you will be with Me in Paradise" (Luke 23:43). The redeemed will see the nail prints in His hands, the marks of the spear in His wounded side, and the compassionate countenance of His glorious face. Jesus will be more lovely than mere words could ever express, and He will be available to heaven's residents throughout eternity!

A great joy for those dwelling in heaven will be the freedom from sinners and their wicked acts. "Then He who sat on the throne said, Behold, I make all things new. And He said to me, Write, for these words are true and faithful. And He said to me, It is done! I am the Alpha and the Omega, the Beginning and the End. I will give of the fountain of the water of life freely to him who thirsts. He who overcomes shall inherit all things, and I will be his God and he shall be My son. But the cowardly, unbelieving, abominable, murders, sexually immoral, sorcerers, idolaters, and all liars shall have their part in the lake which burns with fire and brimstone, which is the second death" (Revelation 21:5-8). The sins listed are certainly not foreign to earth's inhabitants. People live in constant fear and danger from sins committed universally. Sin has ravaged all mankind and, frequently, innocent individuals are harmed, injured, or killed due to sinful acts of others. Although Satan has played havoc with sins that affect essentially everyone, heaven will be free from this torment. Nothing evil nor sad will be found in heaven. "But there shall by no means enter it anything that defiles, or causes an abomination or a lie, but only those who are written in the Lamb's Book of Life" (Revelation 21:27).

The actual architecture of heaven (New Jerusalem, Holy City) is beyond comprehension. The apostle, John, was taken to a high mountain for a prophetic preview of heaven. The precise detail of his description is remarkable. "Then one of the seven angels who had the seven bowls filled with the seven last plagues came to me and talked with me, saying, Come, I will show you the bride, the Lamb's wife. And he carried me away in the Spirit to a great and high mountain, and showed me the great city, the Holy Jerusalem, descending out of heaven from God, having the glory of God. Her light was like a most precious stone, like a jasper stone, clear as crystal. Also she had a great and high wall with 12 gates, and 12 angels at the gates, and names written on them, which are the names of the 12 tribes the children of Israel: three gates on the east, three gates on the north, three gates on the south, and three gates on the west" (Revelation 21:9-13).

John stood in awe as he viewed this heavenly city. He noted the city was lighted with brightness displayed as crystal-clear jasper. An immense wall surrounded the New Jerusalem; this wall had 12 gates, three on each of four sides. Each gate was labeled with the name of one of the 12 tribes of Israel and an angel was posted at each entrance.

The apostle John continued to detail the amazing things he saw. "Now the wall of the city had twelve foundations, and on them were the names of the twelve apostles of the Lamb. And he who talked with me had a gold reed to measure the city, its gates, and its wall. The city is laid out as a square; its length is as great as its breadth. And he measured the city with the reed: twelve thousand furlongs. Its length, breadth, and height are equal. Then he measured its wall: one hundred and forty-four cubits, according to the measure of a man, that is, of an angel. The construction of its wall was of jasper; and the city was pure gold, like clear glass. The foundations of the wall of the city were adorned with all kinds of precious stones: the first foundation was jasper, the second sapphire, the third chalcedony, the fourth emerald, the fifth sardonyx, the sixth sardius, the seventh chrysolite, the eighth beryl, the ninth topaz, the tenth chrysoprase, the eleventh jacinth, and the twelfth amethyst. The twelve gates were twelve pearls: each individual gate was of one pearl. And the street of the city was pure gold like transparent glass" (Revelation 21:14-21).

The wall was made of jasper and it was described as being 144 cubits (216 feet) high. Twelve foundations supported the wall, each layer rendering the name of one of Christ's apostles. The size of the Holy City was determined by using a gold reed. The Heavenly City was 1,500 miles (12,000 furlongs) wide, deep, and high. Thus, the base footprint of the new Holy City will cover ground space equal to one-half of the United States. Construction materials of the wall and city were identified. Each gate in the wall consisted on a single pearl, the city was pure gold like glass and the foundations of its wall were adorned with an abundance of 12 precious stones. Although the greater portion of the foundations of earthly walls are below ground level, these heavenly structures will be visible so all can admire their beauty.

There are several unanswered questions about heaven. Of course, these concerns do not diminish heaven's greatness nor beauty. Why does the Holy City need such high walls? Certainly, God could keep out those who do not belong there. Also, why are angels posted at each gate? Perhaps the high walls and guardian angels are there to remind the redeemed that only those who accepted God's gracious gift of salvation would be welcomed into the Holy City. Gates that are open to all four directions indicate that salvation continues to be readily available to everyone from everywhere who will accept this free gift. Those entering through the wall surrounding heaven will see the name of one of the 12 tribes of Israel written on each of the gates. What a solemn, blessed reminder that God will have chosen Jewish saints from every tribe to spend eternity with him.

What kind of light will be reflected by the walls that are crystal clear transparent jasper? Jasper gemstones are translucent allowing light to pass through them. Thus, these walls will radiate and reflect bright rays of God's divine illumination producing colored lighting for all of heaven's occupants to enjoy. The dimensions of heaven are presented as being equal in width, depth, and height. Some biblical scholars believe that these dimensions could apply to a pyramid rather than a cube. No one has advocated that the Holy City could be a dome rising above the square foundation; however, this would be another possibility. From the apostle John's description, a definitive shape of the New Jerusalem is not provided. This is a small matter for God tells us that He will have space for all his children. "In My Father's house are many mansions; if it were not so, I would have told you" (John 14:2).

Heaven's streets were described as constructed from pure gold that resembled transparent glass. The human mind cannot fathom the concept of pure, transparent gold. Using this precious metal for streets is totally incomprehensible to our finite minds. Gold is relatively soft so how could folks possibly walk on its surfaces continually without destroying the streets. Not to worry, neither can we understand a loving God who would send his only priceless Son to die for those who are sinners. "But God demonstrates His own love toward us, in that while we were still sinners, Christ died for us" (Romans 5:8). No one knows how we will move about on heaven's streets. We may not walk on them but, merely, fly low. Should we walk, we may have nonabrasive feet or the Almighty God who made soft gold could surely make it very rigid.

John continues his description of heaven by providing insights into its inner areas. In addition to transparent golden streets, there is a crystal clear river that originates at the throne of God and flows throughout the Holy City. "And he showed me a pure river of water of life, clear as crystal, proceeding from the throne of God and of the Lamb" (Revelation 22:1). Some believe that the continual flow of this pure river of life symbolizes God's perpetual outflow of blessings to his glorified children.

17

Another item of interest is the tree, or trees, of life that will again be found in the New Jerusalem. "In the middle of its street, and on either side of the river, was the tree of life, which bore twelve fruits, each tree yielding its fruit every month. The leaves of the tree were for healing of the nations" (Revelation 22:2). Various locations for these trees are mentioned, thus, there will likely be many of these in heaven. Adam and Eve sinned originally by eating the forbidden fruit from the tree of life and were driven from the Garden of Eden. During eternity, these trees will again be present in the eternal paradise, providing a variety of fruit for the redeemed saints.

It is easy to allow our minds to wander and question what we will do with our time forever during eternity in heaven. Since there is no night, will people be awake constantly? Surely, heaven's occupants will dwell on eternal values rather than previous earthly temporal problems. Enjoying the tremendous beauty of heaven will, in itself, be a wonderful continuing adventure. We will have unending time to worship God and commune with him. Jesus will be available for frequent interactions. Our loved ones from the past, plus all the great saints from throughout history, will be there for constant companionship, interactions, and enjoyment. No doubt, there will be heavenly choirs singing continually. Certainly, God's children will not be bored in heaven!

Heaven will be an indescribably beautiful and joyful eternal destination for God's redeemed children. This book will focus on the gold, pearls, and gems that will make up the New Jerusalem. As these structural elements are reviewed, an even greater longing for heaven should result. It would be utterly foolish and derelict for anyone to declare disinterest in spending eternity in God's Holy City. But, sadly, there will be many who will not gain entrance into this marvelous eternal home. Readers who are not absolutely assured about their home in the desired destination of heaven should read carefully the last chapter in this book titled, *Heaven, A Decided Destination.* God has prepared a magnificent heavenly future for His prepared people. You'll be forever grateful if you accept God's terms for spending eternity in His blissful city.

Chapter 2
Jasper

The precious stone, jasper, must be a favorite of God. Certainly, heaven will be well-endowed with this gem. The huge wall surrounding the Holy City will be constructed from jasper. One of its foundations will also be adorned with this precious stone plus 11 other highly valued gems. These large jasper walls are described as being clear as crystal, allowing God's special illumination, His divine light to be radiated through them. Indeed, this will be a spectacular luminous display to be enjoyed forever by all of heaven's residents.

Jasper is an ornamental rock consisting of chalcedony and microcrystalline quartz. Additional minerals in this rock produce colorful bands and unique patterns. Minerals include iron, alumina, manganese, and nickel. Patterns observed are spotted, banded, striped, flowery, or diverse irregular silhouettes. Colors of jasper are yellow, brown, red, white, black, and several shades of green and the gem is frequently named by its patterns.

An interesting legend surrounds a variety of jasper, called bloodstone, that is mined in India. This green-colored gem is spotted with red specks. Allegedly, when Christ was crucified, his blood fell to the ground below the cross and stained the emerald-colored rocks. This is an engaging tale; however, bloodstone jasper was known to be valued in India long before Christ's birth and the red spots have been identified as iron oxide. Bloodstone jasper is found primarily in India while other varieties have been discovered in Egypt, Australia, Brazil, Canada, Kazakhstan, Madagascar, Russia, Uruguay, and the United States.

In addition to its use in a large variety of jewelry, jasper has been fashioned into several other decorative items. This gem has been used to make cups, dishes, canisters, bowls, and statuettes. A bloodstone jasper bust of Jesus Christ is located in the French Royal Collection in Paris and a jasper-sculpted head of Jesus is displayed in the Field Columbian Museum in Chicago. Jasper decorates the wall of the Saint Wenceslas Chapel in Prague, and it has been selected as the state rock for Massachusetts.

Hardness of jasper, according to Mohs scale, is 6.5 to 7.0 and it has a specific gravity of 2.58 to 2.91. The refractive index is 1.54 with double refraction of 0.004, both contributing to the brilliant colored light reflected through jasper.

Jasper was a favorite precious stone in ancient days and it is referenced in Greek, Hebrew, Assyrian, and Latin literature. Although current varieties of jasper are essentially all multicolored, many believe that in antiquity this gem may have been green and transparent. This view would certainly substantiate the biblical description of heaven's crystal clear jasper. One can be assured that the variety of jasper appearing eventually in heaven will more than meet every expectation of the redeemed saints. The transmission of God's illumination through the beautiful crystal clear jasper wall of heaven and its foundation will be magnificent.

Chapter 3
Gold

Gems or precious stones will make up the walls surrounding heaven but the Holy City and its streets will be constructed from gold. This will not be ordinary gold as we know it today. The Bible states that this will be pure gold with the appearance of transparent glass. An immense city, measuring 1, 500 miles in length, breadth, and height, made entirely from gold, is beyond human imagination. No current structure nor masses of created or constructed material anywhere on earth come close to duplicating this monumental size.

Gold is identified by the atomic symbol Au which represents the Latin word, Aurum. It is golden yellow in color and has been valued highly throughout history. Gold has the unique qualities of being scarce, indestructible, and easily fashioned. Gold never rusts nor tarnishes, is highly resistant to most chemicals, and can be recycled repeatedly for different uses.

Due to its value, gold-appearing flakes found in rocks have sometimes been confused with true gold. These imitation gold-colored materials are called fools gold and include the sulfides pyrite, chalcopyrite, and marcasite or the mica mineral, biotite. Many times in past history, wars and destruction of civilizations have been precipitated by the conquest for gold.

There are two primary types of gold deposits: lode deposits which consist of veins in cracks among rocks, and placer deposits made up of gold that has washed from lode deposits into streams, among rocks, or beneath the soil. Gold has been found in both California and South Dakota in the United States as well as in the countries of Canada, Mexico, Australia, Russia, Siberia, and South Africa. Discovery of gold at the Sutter Mill in California in 1848 caused a monumental gold rush. During several ensuing years, over 500 million dollars worth of gold was removed from this area. Currently, the largest gold recovery enterprise in the United States is the Homestake Mining Company in Lead, South Dakota. Worldwide, the most important and greatest deposits of gold were discovered in 1886 at Witwatersrand near Johannesburg in South Africa. Here, gold is still recovered from vast rock sheets or reefs which extend to depths of over 13,000 feet in an area stretching hundreds of miles, thus continuing to make South Africa the world's largest gold-producing country. The United States is second in world gold production and Australia is third. It has been estimated that the total amount of gold recovered worldwide by the end of 2002 was approximately 145,000 tons. By far, the greatest reserves of gold are present in ocean waters. It has been estimated that 20 million tons of this prized metal are located in these bodies of water. Unfortunately, the costs for recovering gold from oceans would exceed its value, thus tapping this source has not been pursued.

Five thousand years ago, the Sumerian culture in Mesopotamia was already crafting beautiful jewelry and religious articles from gold. Since this metal is very malleable, it can be cast, carved, drawn out, and hammered into any desired shapes. Approximately one-third of annual gold production is used for jewelry. Since it allows excellent thermal and electrical conductivity, gold is used often for sophisticated industrial applications. The protecting visors used by astronauts are coated with gold to shield their eyes from the sun's high intensity light rays. Further, gold film is applied to spacecraft to reflect damaging infrared rays. Gold is ideal for dental use since it is easy to shape and doesn't corrode in the mouth. Many famous national and international buildings have domes covered with hammered gold leaf.

Gold continues to be the monetary standard used by most nations of the world and many counties have cast coins from this precious metal. When Teddy Roosevelt was President of the United States, he decided that the country's gold coins were unattractive. In 1906 he asked his good friend, sculptor Augustus Saint-Gaudens, to redesign the coins. The result was production of $20 St. Gaudens Double Eagle coins consisting of 90% pure gold. These coins were minted from 1907 through 1933 and, thereafter, another President, Franklin Roosevelt, ordered all St. Gaudens coins to be melted down, depositing the gold in the US Gold Reserves. Thus there are only a limited number of St. Gaudens coins remaining and they are considered as one of the rarest treasures of collectors. Previously, only three of these coins were known to remain in existence, one being sold in 2002 for

7.9 million dollars. Recently, ten more of these rare coins were found. However, the only St. Gaudens coin that may be owned legally is the one sold during the 2002 auction. When production of St. Gaudens Double Eagle coins was discontinued, a slightly varied design was minted which remains highly popular with collectors worldwide. This current coin, called the American Eagle, contains 91.67% gold. Although gold coins are minted worldwide, brick-like gold bars, known as ingots, are generally used in world trade rather than gold coins.

Beaten or hammered gold is mentioned frequently in the Old Testament. Different items or structures were often overlayed with gold to enhance their beauty. Sadly, gold was even used occasionally for the shaping of idols.

For many purposes, gold is too soft for practical use so it is alloyed with other metals such as silver, copper, platinum, or nickel. While these metals cause little change in the color of gold, they effectively harden the end product for many applications. The proportion of gold in jewelry and other items is measured by karats. Pure gold is divided into 24 parts so it is 24 karat. The amount of other material added to gold determines the final karat designation, thus a ring that contains 14 parts of gold and 10 parts of an other material would be 14 karat.

Pure gold measures 2.5 to 3.0 on the Mohs hardness scale, placing it among the softer decorative materials. It has a specific gravity of 19.29 making it heavier than most gems and precious metals; however, it does not have refractive qualities. Gold, as currently known, is opaque and will not permit transmission of light. Occasionally, gold has been hammered into sheets so thin that sunlight will shine through the metal but it does not become transparent.

Although multiple tons of gold have been produced, this quantity would fail to meet the requirements of this precious metal for the massive construction of heaven. This fact will obviously not present a problem to our Eternal God who, after speaking the universe into being, could surely provide the vast stores of gold needed. The gold in heaven will be unlike the beautiful metal we have learned to understand, admire, and value. It will be clear as glass and allow divine illumination from God to shine through. This light, combined with the ember rays emitted from heaven's transparent jasper wall, will be beyond description. Certainly, there will be no darkness nor sorrow there!

Chapter 4
Pearl

Among the precious stones and the one prized metal, gold, an additional item of beauty will comprise heaven's architecture. The 12 gates in the walls surrounding the Holy City will each consist of a single huge pearl. Since no pearl of such magnitude has ever existed on earth, only the facts currently known about this decorative gem can be explored.

Natural pearls are of organic origin, grown in mollusks such as oysters and mussels. When a small grain of sand, or other tiny foreign object, accidentally becomes lodged under the shells of these animals, they secrete a substance called nacre around the irritant material. Nacre consists of a combination of carbonate of lime and organic matter. A pearl enlarges as multiple concentric layers of nacre are deposited to isolate the irritant over a period of several years. The color of the pearl is the same as that of the interior of the mollusk shell under which it develops. Colors range from opaque white through pink, yellow, salmon, fawn, purple, red, green, brown, blue, and black. Light reflecting from these overlapping layers of nacre produces an iridescent brilliance known as orient of pearl.

Natural pearls have been harvested from the Gulf of Manaar of the Indian Ocean, Red Sea, and Persian Gulf. Further, both freshwater and saltwater pearls are found in the waters around Japan and China. Additionally, freshwater pearls are available in the rivers of the United States, Scotland, Ireland, France, Austria, and Germany.

Ninety percent of present day pearls are not natural but cultivated commercially. Cultured pearls are not artificial; however, they are induced by human intervention. Their cost is considerably less than the price of natural pearls. To produce a cultured pearl, a tiny rounded bead, fashioned from mollusk shell, is injected under the shell of another mollusk. Thereafter, a pearl is formed over a period of five to eight years. Cultured pearls are produced primarily off the coasts of Polynesia and Australia. Only about 15 per cent of cultured pearls develop into gem quality. People in the United States have been the primary purchasers of these pearls for many of the past decades. Imitation pearls are produced from painted glass, plastic, or fish scales. These fake gems are fairly easy to identify. It is considerably more difficult to differentiate between natural and cultured pearls; x-radiation must be employed for this purpose.

Pearls are the most highly valued of all organic gems and have long been known as the Queen of Gems. They are the only ornamental objects that do not require reworking or polishing before use. Pearls vary considerably in size, the smallest measures less than the diameter of the head of a pin. The largest pearl is located in the Museum at South Kensington, London and weighs three ounces with a length of two inches and a circumference of four and a half inches.

Pearls are generally sized in either in karats or grains. Seventy per cent of pearls are strung and worn as necklaces. They have been used for jewelry more than 6,000 years and there was considerable pearl trade in China as early as 2,500 BC. The pearl has been selected as the official birthstone for the month of June.

The most valuable pearls are spherical while those that are asymmetrical, or baroque, have lower values. Pearls are fairly soft and range between 2.50 and 4.50 on the Mohs scale of hardness. Their specific gravity ranges from 2.60 to 2.85, they have a refractive index of 1.52 to 1.69, and double refraction of 0.16. The softer pearls can be scratched or damaged quite easily. Pearls undergo slow deterioration if exposed to acids, cosmetics, hair spray, perspiration, or either low or high humidity levels. Surfaces initially become dull or discolored and, eventually, fissures appear and further disintegration occurs. The life of pearls ranges from 100 to 150 years. Unfortunately, restoration of damaged pearls is difficult and often unsuccessful. Proper care of pearls involves wiping them carefully with a clean soft cloth after use, wrapping them in fabric, and storing them in a closed container.

God's provision of gate-sized pearls in the walls surrounding heaven is surely of great interest. Pearls of this size have never been seen and are unknown to mankind. Also, the huge pearls will not deteriorate over eons of time. Their high double refraction values should make them appear bright and luminous as light reflects from their surfaces. What a wonderful experience awaits those who will enter these unique and spectacular iridescent light-reflecting gates.

Chapter 5
Sapphire

Sapphires are part of the corundum group of rocks. These rocks consist of the crystalline form of aluminum oxide. The rough corundum rocks are mined, cut, and polished into sparkling gemstones. The precise art required in cutting these stones brings out the best color displays. The red gems in the corundum rock group are known as rubies while all other colors are sapphires. Although, there are no shortages of sapphires worldwide, gems of highest quality are rare and costly. Blue gems are the most commonly observed sapphires, being royal blue, velvet blue, or the favorite, cornflower blue. Cashmere sapphires display pure and intensive blue coloring with a silky gloss and are considered the most beautiful and valuable of these gemstones. Any of the blue sapphires may be termed oriental by gem dealers. Bright sunlight produces increased radiance in sapphires and a few are nearly transparent allowing transmission of brilliantly colored light rays.

Sapphires that are other than blue are termed fancy. These colors include gems that are yellow, green, black, white, orange, pink, and brown. Yellow sapphires may be called oriental topaz and the green gems are known as oriental peridot. There are colorless sapphires and orange-pink sapphires have been found, called padparadshas, which means lotus flowers. Color of sapphires is deepened by exposing them to high temperatures. Heat treatments also remove some minor blemishes found in these gems. Sapphires containing tiny needle-like mineral deposits display a star-shaped appearance; this optical property is called asterism. When these gems are cut into smooth domes, they present a star with six, nine or, occasionally, 12 rays. Rarely, sapphires are found that display a cat's eye effect called chatoyancy. This variance occurs in stones when a small band of light is reflected back from the center of the sapphire. Artificial sapphires have been created in laboratories and are difficult to distinguish from naturally formed gems.

The best quality sapphires are found in Ceylon, Thailand, Australia, India, Burma, Africa, and Brazil, and attractive blue metallic sapphires have been mined in the United States in Montana. The largest star sapphire was found in Burma in 1966, weighing over 28 pounds. Other large sapphires include the Star of India and the Midnight Star in The American Museum of Natural History in New York, the Star of Asia in the Smithsonian Institution in Washington, DC, and the St. Edwards and Stuart Sapphires in the English Crown Jewels display in London. The heads of Presidents Washington, Lincoln. and Eisenhower have been carved from large sapphires, all located in the United States.

Sapphires are popular in all types of jewelry settings. Many women treasure them for engagement rings since they allegedly symbolize loyalty and faithfulness. Sapphires have also been associated with emotions such as friendship, harmony, and sympathy. In addition to being designated as the birthstone for the month of September, they have been suggested as special gifts for the 5th, 23rd, 45th, and 65th wedding anniversaries. According to legend, the Ten Commandments God presented to Moses were inscribed on sapphire tablets. However, there is no scriptural verification of this legend.

Sapphires rate 8.0 to 9.0 on the Mohs scale of hardness, second only to diamonds which are harder and grade 10.0. They have specific gravity is 3.95 to 4.03, a refraction index of 1.76 to 1.79, and double refraction of 0.008. Because of their hardness, sapphires may be cleaned with ultrasonic cleaners, steamers, soapy water, and brushes. Since these gems are very hard, they should not be stored with other jewelry that could be scratched easily. Accidental high impact to sapphires may cause surface damage or produce cracks.

Ancient civilizations have recorded information indicating that their sapphires were blue. This is still the preferred color of these gems and may actually be the color that the apostle John described as garnishing the second foundation of heaven's wall. If the sapphire-enhanced foundation of the Holy City should have transparent qualities, its beauty would be increased even further. Sapphires are highly prized and beautiful gemstones; won't heaven be wonderful?

Chapter 6
Chalcedony

Chalcedony, also known as agate, is composed of minute, dense, quartz crystals. These gems are formed in concentric layers while the crystals fill cavities in host rocks. They must be examined under a microscope to view their crystalline structures. Chalcedony gems have exterior surfaces that display a waxy luster and they vary from being translucent to transparent

Colors of chalcedony include white, gray, blue, and brown. Contrasting bands of colors and moss or tree-like images are found in many of these gems. Inclusions of impurities, such as iron pigments and carbon, produce the different colors and images. Chalcedony is porous and can, therefore, be dyed easily to exhibit assorted colors. The dyed gems are generally indistinguishable from natural stones. Banded chalcedony will undergo permanent color changes when exposed to heat or acid treatments. In the jewelry market, these gems do not need to be identified as having been subjected to color changing processes.

Abundant supplies of chalcedony are available worldwide with deposits found in virtually every continent. One of the most famous deposits of this rock is located in the vicinity of Idar-Oberstein, Germany, where collection has continued since 1548. Organic material in petrified wood is frequently replaced by chalcedony. A notable amount of such fossilized wood is found in the Petrified Forests in Arizona. This gem rates 6.0 to 7.0 on the Mohs scale of hardness. It has a density of 2.58 to 2.64, refractive index of 1.53 to 1.54, and double refraction of 0.004 to 0.009.

Chalcedony was a favorite gem among ancient peoples. It is easy to process and polish and remains valued today. Chalcedony is sometimes displayed as thin rock slabs or it may be used as ornaments, rings, cameos, brooches, necklaces, or pendants. Folk tales indicated that this gem produced emotional balance, vitality, stamina, endurance, kindness, charity, and friendship. Further, this gem was supposed to reduce hostility, irritability, and melancholy moods. Should any of these anecdotes be true, exploitation of current reserves would certainly result in a short supply of this gem.

There may be several colors of chalcedony in the third foundation of heaven's wall. Some of these gems are translucent or transparent so light should be transmitted through them readily. With average refractive indexes and double refraction values, the light rays would bend in several directions. The light displays and reflections caused by chalcedony will certainly further enhance the beauty of heaven.

Chapter 7
Emerald

The fourth foundation of heaven's wall will be garnished with emeralds. These are fascinating gemstones that radiate an intense light green color described as that of fresh young grass. The elegant coloring results from small amounts of chromium and iron in these gems. The name, emerald, is derived from the Greek word smaragdos, which means green stone. Some emeralds exhibit either blue or yellow tones and only a few of the very best specimens are transparent. The hue of emeralds changes between sunlight and artificial illumination. Most contain inclusions called jardin, which are primarily calcite deposits. Jardin is a French word which means garden, and this term is used since emerald inclusions resemble intricate plant forms. Inclusions in these gemstones are not considered as negative aspects but, rather, add to the character and authenticity of emeralds. Flawless emeralds are seldom found so most are vacuum and heat treated with oil or epoxy resin fillers to disguise cracks, hide defects, enhance color, and reduce the risk of fractures. These treatments are considered acceptable by gem dealers; however, dying them to change colors is unacceptable unless disclosed.

Quality emeralds are scarce and command high prices, many are more expensive than fine diamonds. Due to their great value and popularity, synthetic or fake gems are frequently marketed as emeralds. Imitation gems are made from glass, fashioned with commonly observed flaws to make them appear authentic. Although often difficult to differentiate, natural gems can be distinguished from fake jewels by exposing them to ultraviolet light. Synthetic fraudulent stones reflect the ultraviolet light whereas natural gems fail to do so.

Emeralds are used frequently for jewelry. including rings, cameos, cabochons (non-faceted convex stones), and beads. They have been designated as the birthstone for the month of May. Large emeralds are displayed in several museums worldwide. Gems weighing several hundred karats are located in the British Museum of Natural History in London, the American Museum of Natural History in New York, and in the treasuries of Russia, Iran, and Turkey.

Emeralds are found in small veins within rocks, the host rock often being limestone. They were among of the first gems mined by the ancient Egyptians, and it is thought that Cleopatra's Mines were the oldest source for these precious stones. Currently, only poor quality emeralds are found in these mines. Presently, the highest quality gems are mined in Colombia around the city of Bogotá while other sources are Austria, India, Australia, South Africa, Pakistan, and Zimbabwe. An extremely rare cat's eye emerald that displays six-spoked stars was found in Brazil. Formerly, emeralds were found in North Carolina in the United Sates but their supply has been exhausted.

Emeralds rate 7.5 to 8.0 on Mohs scale of hardness, have a refraction index of 1.57 to 1.60, double refraction of 0.004 to 0.008, and specific gravity of 2.67 to 2.78. Brittleness and the presence of fissures makes cutting of emeralds difficult and risky. To prevent excess loss or damage, a special design called the emerald cut is used. This results in a rectangular gem with beveled corners, bringing out its beauty and protecting the stone from mechanical stress. In the natural state, emeralds crack easily but they are quite resistant to chemicals. Since most emeralds undergo surface sealing treatments, they should not be cleaned in ultrasonic cleaners nor should strong cleansing agents be used.

The history of emeralds goes back to antiquity. It is thought that these gems may have been included in the jewelry the Egyptians gave the Israelites as they fled from bondage. The beautiful green gems of our day are believed to be similar to those seen by the apostle John during his preview of heaven. These radiant stones, some being transparent, with their refraction indices should radiate captivating directional green rays from both the transmission and reflection of light. Where, but in heaven, would such elegance be seen?

Chapter 8
Sardonyx

Sardonyx, also called onyx, is part of the chalcedony mineral group of precious stones. The gem consists of several stacked layers of tiny quartz fibers resulting in a banded appearance. Ranging from opaque to translucent, these precious stones are usually reddish-brown in color interspersed with white bands. Because of their beauty they are sometimes called the fancy wallpaper of nature. In the apostle John's vision, he described the fifth foundation of heaven's wall as enriched with sardonyx.

Sardonyx has also been called the gem of courage since it allegedly inspired orators and lovers. Further, it was formerly used for protection against warts, boils, cramps, the evil eye, wicked thoughts, and the activity of witches. In ancient days, the Egyptians engraved these gems to resemble beetles. Wearing them was thought to bring good luck. Roman soldiers carried sardonyx stones engraved with Mars, their god of war, believing these artifacts increased bravery during battles.

The best sardonyx gems are found in India while those of lesser quality have been discovered in Germany, Czechoslovakia, Brazil, Uruguay, and the United States in the Lake Superior region and in Oregon. These stones are formed through deposition of silica within gas cavities that are located in lava. With hardness of 7.0 on the Mohs scale, this gem has a refractive index of 1.53 to 1.54, double refraction of 0.004, and specific gravity of 2.61.

Sardonyx is relatively common and inexpensive, making it readily available to those of average means. These gemstones have been designated as the birthstone for August. In the current jewelry market, sardonyx is most often used for beads and to a lesser extent for brooches, cameos, and intaglios. Cameos are produced by carving figures in the top light-colored layers of the gems contrasting with the darker underlying base layers. Intaglios consist of the opposite color configurations displaying the darker figures in the top layers. Currently, most cameos and intaglios are engraved in Paris and Italy. Sardonyx gems should be cleaned with a soft polishing cloth, followed with a light application of olive oil to enhance their brilliance.

An interesting tale is told about a cameo involving Queen Elizabeth I of England. Apparently, a beautiful sardonyx stone, carved to resemble the Queen, was set in a gold ring. She presented the ring to the Earl of Essex as a token of friendship and support. Thereafter, the Earl was imprisoned for treason and later beheaded. Prior to his death, he attempted to send the ring back to the Queen. However, it fell into the hands of Lady Nottingham whose husband greatly disliked the Earl. During Lady Nottingham's deathbed confession to the Queen regarding the ring, it is alleged that the Queen shook the dying countess exclaiming, "God may forgive you, but I cannot!"

Sardonyx that will embellish the foundation of the wall surrounding heaven will consist of opaque to translucent reddish-brown stones laced with white bands. The yellow illumination from the Holy City should display orange colored rays in multiple directions as it passes through these red-tinted translucent gems. This is yet another pleasing color of light that will be displayed in heaven. With each successive foundation, the beauty of light reflections and transmissions will be increasingly spectacular.

Chapter 9
Sardius

The sixth foundation of heaven is decorated with sardius, the term derived from the Greek word, sardios. These stones, also known as carnelian, range in color from clear orange-red to dark orange-brown and vary from being translucent to transparent. They consist of microscopic, slender parallel bands of quartz crystals. When exposed to sunlight, the color of these gemstones changes to red. The highest quality sardius is translucent and deep red in color, the red tint caused by the presence of iron oxide.

Ancient Egyptian tombs contain numerous carnelian jewels since this culture believed the gem provided power during the afterlife. In early days, it was thought that sardius potions sedated the blood and calmed tempers. There are also records from ancient literature that these stones, when worn, prevented skin diseases and insanity, bestowed motivation and eloquence, enhanced public speaking, produced relaxation, intensified love relation-ships, relieved depression and grief, soothed arthritis, and strengthened numerous body systems. There is still the belief today that, by keeping this gem near one's body, sardius will protect against poverty and encourage a sense of humor. If true, these last two related results should energize everyone to purchase these precious stones immediately.

Sardius is found in Australia, China, India, Sri Lanka, Brazil, Uruguay, and California. From Victorian times, sardius has been used primarily for engraved jewelry such as cameos and intaglios. It is also polished for beads, crafted into sculptures, carved for rings and wax seals, and used for various inlay designs. The hardness of sardius ranges from 6.5 to 7.0 on the Mohs scale and this gem has a specific gravity of 2.59 to 2.65, refractive index of 1.53 to 1.54, and double refraction of 0.004.

Quality sardius gems that are translucent and deep red in color may well be similar to those present in the sixth foundation of heaven's wall. God's glory shining through the golden Holy City should result in the transmission and reflection of brilliant orange deflected light rays, caused by the refractive index and double refraction of these gemstones. What a magnificent sight this must have been as the apostle John gazed upon the resplendent wall of heaven.

Chapter 10
Chrysolite

The seventh foundation of heaven's wall will be enhanced with chrysolite. This gem is commonly called peridot by current day jewelers. In the arena of mineralogy, chrysolite is called olivine due to its olive-green color. These gemstones are composed of silicate of magnesia plus traces of iron oxide. They are usually rich yellow-green in color, display a vitreous and greasy appearance, and are transparent to translucent

Chrysolite is found in volcanic rocks and is also present in meteors that have fallen to the earth. The gems have been discovered in Australia, Brazil, Kenya, Mexico, Sri Lanka, South Africa, Tanzania, Norway, and Arizona in the United States. The finest stones were found as recently as 1994 in Pakistan, many being large in size with one weighing over 300 karats. The largest chrysolite stone weighs 310 karats and is located in the Smithsonian Institution in Washington, DC. Several cut chrysolite gems are located in Russia. They were collected from a meteorite that fell in Eastern Siberia in 1749.

Multiple legends exist about the powers and uses of chrysolite. Beads were strung in the hair of a donkey, as well as tied to a person's left arm, to ward off evil spirits. Attaching the gem to the left arm also protected the wearer from the evil eye. The stone was used to encourage friendship and was thought to remove envious thoughts from one's mind, probably the reason it would produce friendship. Several other mythical attributes of chrysolite included the bringing of good luck, peace, and success; provision of good health and peaceful sleep; power to attract love and calm anger; and the ability to sooth nerves and remove negative emotions.

Currently, some Mexican tribes still drink from chrysolite cups in an attempt to communicate with their ancestor's spirits. American Indians living in Arizona mix ground peyote with crystals from these gems for use in their secret rituals. In South America, the Shamans wear this stone to avoid snake bites. Chrysolite was alleged to be one of the favorite gemstones of Queen Cleopatra of Egypt. The breast plates of King Solomon and of the High Priest Aaron were described as decorated with chrysolite stones to protect them from injury and death during battles. Further, it is recorded that Solomon traded cedar trees from Lebanon for cups fashioned from chrysolite.

Chrysolite was brought by the Crusaders from the Mediterranean region during the Middle Ages and used to decorate European cathedrals. Many of these decorative displays may still be seen today. Large stones over 200 karats in size also beautify the shrine of the three magi at the Cologne Cathedral in Germany. Chrysolite, designated as the birthstone for the month of August, is used for various pieces of jewelry and it remains highly popular among American Indians. Imitations of these gems are produced from corundum, spinel, and evergreen bottle glass.

Chrysolite has a hardness of 6.5 to 7.0 on Mohs scale, density of 3.28 to 3.48, refractive index of 1.65 to 1.70, and double refraction of 0.036 to 0.038. Among gemstones, chrysolite has one of the highest double refraction index values. Chrysolite should be handled with care because it is quite soft and scratches or breaks fairly easily. Further, this gem may be damaged by abrasive substances and most acids.

Transparent to translucent olive-green chrysolite gems will be placed in the seventh foundation of heaven's wall. With a high double refraction value, light passing through and reflecting from these gemstones will present brilliant dancing waves of illumination. While these waves interact with all the other multicolored, multidirectional light rays from the wall, this marvelous exhibition will be beyond human imagination.

Chapter 11
Beryl

Beryl is the gem that the apostle John saw embellishing the eighth foundation of the wall that will surround heaven. These crystals may be transparent to translucent and consist of beryllium-aluminum-silicates. Beryl was originally named after the Greek term, beryllos, which means precious blue color. Since then, several other colors of beryl have been recognized. Aquamarine is a popular beryl that is sea-blue in color, deriving its name from the Latin term aqua marina which means sea water. Minute amounts of iron content cause this variety to display a slight green sparkle. This gem may form extremely large crystals weighing as much as 200 pounds. Essentially all aquamarine stones have been heat treated to enhance their colors.

Bixbit is a gooseberry-red form of beryl that is found in the United States. The presence of manganese causes the intense red color in this rare and expensive stone. Golden beryl varies in color from lemon to golden yellow and this gem is found in Madagascar, Namibia, Nigeria, Zimbabwe, and Sri Lanka. Goshenite is colorless beryl found in Brazil, China, Canada, Mexico, Russia, and the United States. Clear stones have little economic value, but they may be changed in color to an intense yellow, called golden beryl, when they absorb small traces of iron and uranium. Dark blue beryls, found in the jewelry trade today, are clear gems that were exposed to radiation. Occasionally, colorless beryl is sold as imitation diamonds or emeralds by attaching colored metal foil behind the stones.

Heliodar is a weak-colored yellow-green beryl discovered in 1919 in Namibia. Morganite, a light pink beryl, derives its color from its manganese content. This gem is sometimes heat treated to amplify its pink color. Morganite is found in Afghanistan, Brazil, China, Madagascar, Mozambique, Namibia, Zimbabwe, and the United States. An additional gem that belongs to the beryl group is the emerald. This stone is described previously in Chapter 7 in this book.

Since available in several attractive colors, beryl is used for most types of jewelry. These gems are among the more valuable accessories worn by both modern day women and men. Beryl has been employed for several technological applications including its use in nuclear reactors, an ingredient of rocket fuel, and a component in neon signs. The crystals have been used to strengthen parts used in aerospace equipment, bicycles, and fishing rods.

In ancient times, colorless beryl was used for lenses in eyeglasses. It has been conjectured that the German word for spectacles, brille, may have come from the word beryl. Several ancient legends describe the value of beryl. Wearing this gem allegedly made one resistant to injuries from battles or failures from litigation. Possessing this stone supposedly caused an individual to be friendly, likable, intellectual, and industrious. Greek physicians soaked beryl in water, using the liquid to treat kidney and bladder stones. During the Middle Ages, doctors believed these gems would relieve gas, asthma, and liver problems, plus they were considered effective in providing protection against poisonings, disputes, and marital discord.

Beryl ranks 7.5 to 8.0 on the Mohs scale of hardness, has a specific gravity of 2.63 to 2.89, a refractive index of 1.56 to 1.60, with double refraction of 0.004 to 0.010. The hardness of beryl protects it against damage and, therefore, makes it an ideal gem for jewelry. Hardness also makes these gemstones highly resistant to most detergents and chemicals.

There will be blue to green transparent to translucent beryl stones in the eighth foundation of heaven's wall. The golden illumination from heaven, combined with the blue-green color of beryl, should result in an extraordinary display of emerald green rays. This exceptional array of glittering light will be available to heaven's residents forever.

Chapter 12
Topaz

The ninth foundation of heaven's wall is adorned with the well-known gemstone, topaz. This stone may have received its name from the place where it was found initially. Early discovery of topaz was made on an island in the Red Sea formerly called Topazos, now known as Zebirget. These gemstones are found in igneous rocks and volcanic lava and are composed of silicate of alumina plus hydroxyl and fluorine minerals. Topaz stones consist of hard transparent to translucent crystals that are available in several colors including yellow, light blue, orange, pink, and colorless. A highly preferred gem, called Imperial, is yellow-orange with a tinge of peach or red coloring.

In the 19th century, a pink variety of topaz was discovered in Russia. This gemstone was so highly coveted that only the Czar's family and those with whom they shared this stone were given ownership. In early history, when worn as a charm, topaz was thought to eliminate sadness and increase intellect. When ground into powder and added to wine, this stone was considered effective for curing insomnia, controlling hemorrhage, relieving asthma, and treating burns. During the Middle Ages, topaz was lauded as capable of healing physical and mental illnesses. The Greeks thought that wearing this gem would protect them from injury and could make them become invisible. The Romans were convinced that Topaz had the power to improve their eyesight. Additionally, at that time, topaz was thought to change color in the presence of poisoned food or drink.

Topaz is mined in Brazil, Mexico, China, Sri Lanka, and Africa. Highly prized Imperial Topaz, currently found only in Brazil and Sri Lanka, is in short supply and may no longer be available in the near future. Beautiful topaz stones are held in the Green Vault in Dresden, Germany; the American Museum of Natural History in New York City; the Smithsonian Institution in

Washington, DC, and the British Museum in London. A famous topaz, the 1680 karat Braganza Diamond, is part of the Portuguese Crown Jewels. This gem was originally thought to be a diamond but later identification techniques determined that it was actually a colorless topaz. In 1964, several large blue topaz stones, each weighing over 200 pounds, were found in the Ukraine.

Topaz has been designated as the birthstone for the month of November. The blue variety is most often used in jewelry. Small amounts of these blue stones are mined; however, most seen today are colorless or pale gems that have been exposed to gamma or electron irradiation, followed with heat treatments to stabilize their colors. Colors produced by these treatments are marketed as London Blue, Sky Blue, Swiss Blue, and Maxi Blue. The values of these gems escalate as the intensity of the blue color increases. Early in 1998, a new surface-enhanced topaz entered the jewelry market. These gems are blue to green-blue or emerald green in color. A stone sold as Smoky Topaz is an imitation of true topaz and composed of quartz rather than silicates.

Topaz gems are hard measuring 8.0 on the Mohs scale. They have a specific gravity of 3.49 to 3.57, refractive index of 1.60 to 1.64, and double refraction of 0.008 to 0.016. Because of their hardness, these gems take a high polish but they must be handled with care due to the possibilities of division or splitting. Their above average specific gravity makes them heavier than most precious stones.

Bible scholars believe the topaz in heaven's wall will be transparent yellow-green in color. If true, heaven's bright yellow light rays will penetrate these gems and produce a light emerald green illumination outside the wall for all entrants to envision. Yet another lovely gem, topaz, will provide beautiful lighting for God's redeemed saints

Chapter 13
Chrysoprase

Chrysoprase gems, the rarest and most valued variety of chalcedony, are translucent apple green in color and consist of finely grained quartz microcrystals. The green coloring is caused by the presence of nickel within the stones. Frequently, chrysoprase gems are dyed to enhance their colors. These stones have a hardness of 6.5 to 7.0 on the Mohs scale, specific gravity of 2.58 to 2.64, refractive index of 1.53 to 1.54, and double refraction of 0.004 to 0.009.

Alexander the Great supposedly placed chrysoprase in his girdle during battles to ensure victories. Many legends surround the use and attributes of chrysoprase. Reproductive maladies were reportedly alleviated by remaining near chrysoprase gems. These stones were thought to clarify problems and provide solutions for those in management positions. They were alleged to enhance inner courage, self-confidence, and improve social interactions. Children were encouraged to wear chrysoprase to assist them in solving life's problems and avoiding distractions. Placing a bowl of these gems in a home ensured that those in the dwelling would remain happy.

Early Greek sailors wore chrysoprase charms to protect them from drowning. According to Roman folklore, these gems allowed wearers to understand the language of lizards, which would currently hardly be considered an immense advantage. During the 1800s, thieves were convinced that, by placing these stones in their mouths, they would be rendered invisible instantly. Likely, this belief resulted in many surprised and disappointed reactions from captured robbers.

Chrysoprase is found embedded in hydrated magnesium silicate rock. The highest quality gems come from Queensland, Australia, while others are found in California, Brazil, Austria, and Russia. The highly valued gems obtained from Australia are sometimes called Australian Jade.

The Greeks, Romans, and Egyptians used chrysoprase for jewelry and other ornamental objects. Currently, most of these stones are used as cabochons or for beads in necklaces. The color of these gems may fade from sunlight or heat; however, it is restored quickly by warmth and moisture. Generally, wearing chrysoprase while bathing will restore its natural color. These stones are very durable and are resistant to chipping and cracking. Treating them with olive oil will enhance their brilliance. Occasionally, dealers misrepresent these gems and sell them as more expensive jade.

In the past, chrysoprase has been used to decorate famous buildings. Structures displaying these luxurious gems are the Wencelaus Chapel in Prague, Czechoslovakia, and the Sanssouci Castle in Potsdam, Germany.

Nearing the top of heaven's wall, chrysoprase will brighten the tenth foundation. With its apple green translucent attributes, pale amber reflective light rays will radiate outward from the wall. Along with all the other comely light colors, indeed this will be a splendid vista to behold.

Chapter 14
Jacinth

Jacinth has been available since antiquity and has, over the years, been identified by several different names. Originally known as jacinth, it has since been called hyacinth and, currently is generally referred to as zircon. These brilliant gems are transparent to translucent and are composed of silicate of zirconia. Although many different colored zircon stones exist, jacinth is generally referred to as the orange-red and red-brown varieties. These gems will enrich the eleventh foundation of heaven's wall.

As with most gemstones, during early history several mythical useful benefits were described for jacinth. When worn by women, these stones allegedly assisted them during childbirth. When used by men, these gems prevented bad dreams, protected against lightning, strengthened bodies, fortified heart action, restored appetite, suppressed accumulation of fat, produced sleep, encouraged prosperity, promoted honor and wisdom, and removed grief and sadness.

Jacinth is present as small grains in acidic igneous rocks and alluvial deposits. High quality gemstones have been found in Sri Lanka for over 2,000 years. Other sources of these gems are Australia, Brazil, Cambodia, France, Myanmar, Thailand, Tanzania, Vietnam, and the United States. These stones frequently contain traces of radioactive elements, namely uranium and thorium. Jacinth measures 6.5 to 7.5 on the Mohs scale of hardness, has a specific gravity of 3.93 to 4.73, refractive index of 1.81 to 2.02, and double refraction of 0.002 to 0.059. Due to its high refractive index, this gem shows great brilliance and intense fire. It is one of the heaviest among gemstones. Since it is a very hard brittle stone, it is subject to fractures and chipping.

Jacinth jewelry has been popular in Sri Lanka and India for centuries; however, this stone did not gain acceptance in western countries until the

1920s. It is used for rings, earrings, pendants, and brooches. These gems should be stored separate from other jewelry since their faceted edges may wear or chip and their hard composition may scratch other stones. As a result of these concerns, when these gemstones are incorporated into jewelry, they are generally displayed in protective metal settings. Care should be exercised while cleaning and polishing jacinth since it may be damaged by strong detergents and most acids.

Jacinth will adorn the eleventh foundation of heaven's wall and these gems will likely range from orange to red and brown. Their high refractive indices, transparency, and lavish brilliance will certainly be visible high on the wall. Perhaps, this lovely display of colored lighting will cause heaven's occupants to look up and give praise to their Almighty God. Also, one may be impressed by the fact that, the closer one gets to God's throne, the better it gets!

Chapter 15
Amethyst

The top or twelfth foundation of heaven's wall will be decorated with amethyst gemstones. In order for a gem to be an amethyst, it must be some shade of purple. These stones range in color from pale lilac to lavender, mauve, and deep purple. The pale variety contains manganese and has been known as Rose de France, which was popular in Victorian jewelry. The amounts of iron content within these gems account for the depth of purple coloring. Some amethyst stones contain assorted inclusions that appear as tiger stripes, feathers, or thumb prints. Most of these gems are heat treated to create deeper colors. Once treated in this manner the resulting intensified colors remain permanent. The most highly valued amethyst is deep medium purple, displaying rose-colored flashes. Stones found in Siberia are considered to possess the greatest richness and depth of color.

The Greek word amethystos, from which the term amethyst was derived, meant freedom from drunkenness. Thus, in that day, amethyst was considered as an effective antidote against drunkenness. Amethyst was a favorite of Catherine the Great and the Egyptian royalty. The signet ring of Cleopatra contained an amethyst. Fine representatives of these gems are found among the British Crown Jewels. Amethyst measures 7.0 on the Mohs scale of hardness, with specific gravity of 2.6 to 2.7, refractive index of 1.54 to 1.55, and double refraction of 0.009.

Leonardo Da Vinci described the benefits of amethyst as dissipating evil thoughts and quickening intelligence. Other alleged attributes of these gems include healing of hearing disorders, curing insomnia, treating headaches and pain, eliminating mental disorders, and preventing contagious diseases. Additional virtues of these stones were making the wearer more gentle and agreeable, causing happiness, providing spiritual enlightenment, amplifying dreams, ensuring peace, enhancing love, giving courage, and protecting against thieves, hailstorms, and locusts. Further, by engraving a circle of the sun or moon on this gem, it was thought to prevent death from poisoning.

Amethyst is a transparent variety of quartz and is found in alluvial deposits or in geodes in many parts of the world. Brazil has the largest geodes that contain amethysts. These gems are also found in Russia, Canada, Sri Lanka, India, Uruguay, Madagascar, Germany, Australia, Namibia, Zambia, and the United States. They occur as prismatic crystals with six-sided pyramid ends or they may form as crystalline stones with pointed ends.

Amethysts have been described as being among the most beautiful gemstones available at reasonable prices. The modest prices are due, largely, to the abundance of these stones throughout the world. Amethyst gems are used for all types of jewelry, and they have been designated as the official birthstone for the month of February. Synthetic amethyst is abundant, being fashioned from glass and corundum.

At the upper level of heaven's foundations, the transparent purple amethyst gems will interact with God's golden illumination. This should result in luminous blue-green light transmissions and reflections. These glorious light rays will extend outward from heaven's magnificent wall. Above the wall's array of heavenly lighting, the glorious golden Holy City will be visible. How could anyone resist entrance into this engaging eternal home?

Chapter 16
Gems of Heaven

The Bible provides considerable information about gems. Thus, it appears fitting that the last chapter, Revelation, continues revealing information about precious stones, gold, and pearls. Further, God appears to love gems since he will beautify our heavenly eternal home with massive displays of these highly valued treasures.

Previous scriptural references about gems are interesting. When the Israelites left their years of agonizing bondage under the Egyptians, they departed with an abundance of their enslavers' costly jewels (Exodus 12:35-36). Surely, the mistreated Children of Israel received well-deserved, unexpected delayed payments for some of their distressful sorrowful services. Little did they know that these items would be of value to them later for adornment of priestly garments as well as for decorative garnishment during construction of the Tabernacle and Temple. No doubt, the Israelites mused often about their sad plight in Egypt but God had not forgotten them. They received the very gifts needed for future purposes. Today, although not always seen at the time, God is still involved in caring tenderly and providing abundantly for His children's current and future needs.

It didn't take long for the Children of Israel to realize why God had given them the Egyptians' jewelry. Moses instructed them about the need for a Tabernacle to worship the Lord (Exodus 36:13-38). The wandering Israelites complied immediately with this request and willingly contributed their precious jewels for adornment of the Tabernacle. Why would they part with the most valuable possessions they had to build a worship center? Obviously, they saw the need and decided to obey Moses in providing an appropriate place to worship the mighty God who had delivered them from slavery. Not unlike today, people still give unselfishly for God's causes and worship centers.

God does not look unfavorably toward beauty or items required to produce a pleasing setting for His worship. He allowed the garments of the Old Testament priests to be adorned with many precious gems (Exodus, chapters 28-29). Even now, God does not condemn ownership or use of precious gemstones and other valuable materials. He does however, expect His children to use them wisely and with discernment. Further, He condemns those demonstrating excessive love for these items, and describes the dire consequences resulting from showing an excess desire for riches (1 Timothy 6:10). Because precious jewels were an indication of riches in the Israelite's lives, they recognized their responsibilities to obey God's commands regarding riches. Indeed, it appears they passed the test of giving by making willing contributions of valued items for building the Tabernacle as well as for decorating the priest's garments.

How much emphasis on beauty is too much as far as God is concerned? Reviewing the architecture and furnishings of Solomon's Temple it appears that, for the Lord, the very best is appropriate. Certainly, this resplendent Old Testament Temple left little to be desired in the realm of elegance (Chronicles 29, 2 Chronicles 2-4). Currently, the magnificent cathedrals found worldwide do not eclipse the glory of the Old Testament Temple built under the reign of King Solomon. Obviously, God approves of man's provision of superb edifices for his worship and praise. Surely, that fact should be unmistakable when the construction materials of the Holy City are evaluated.

In reviewing the gems of heaven, it is interesting to note that a few precious jewels, greatly adored in this life, are not included in the description of heaven's construction. There is no mention of diamonds nor silver in heaven. Why not is unknown but, be assured, God knows and we can inquire regarding his reasons when we reach the New Jerusalem. With the massive display of gems that will be in heaven, the absence of diamonds and silver will likely be a moot consideration. There will be more than an adequate collection of gems for all of God's redeemed to enjoy throughout eternity.

Previous chapters have detailed much of what is known about the various precious stones, gold, and pearls. Should any of these facts from our current knowledge differ from heaven's eventual architecture, the correct versions of God's building materials will surely satisfy fully all of heaven's population. In fact, additional conjecture about heaven's gems should increase the anticipation of occupying our future home in the Holy City.

The apostle John describes the immense wall surrounding heaven as having 12 foundations. Whether he counted these from the bottom up or from the top down is not known, nor does it really matter. However, by describing them from one through 12 indicates they were aligned in a specific order. It would appear likely that the first foundation adorned with jasper that John observed was at the bottom since the wall itself was constructed from jasper. Thus he would probably not have described a separate foundation composed of this gem had it not been specifically distinguished from the jasper wall.

The transparent gold construction of the New Jerusalem and its streets is of considerable interest. In our day, gold that is clear like glass is unknown. Such gold would allow glowing light to pass through heaven's walls freely. Thus, the glorious light emanating from God's throne will flood all of heaven and the surrounding area. Its yellow-tinted brilliance will sparkle and interact with the many colored rays reflected from heaven's walls, creating a marvelous light show. Since there will be no night in the Holy City, at no time will any resident be without a constant reminder of the nearness and sustaining power of the Almighty God.

Where could God possibly find the massive amounts of gold needed to build a 1,500-mile square city plus paving its accompanying streets? Allowing even a second of worry over this dilemma is absurd. The God who created the immense universe will have no problem creating gold instantly. If he could speak and throw millions of stars and planets into space, generating huge supplies of transparent gold is a non-problem. Yes, the gold will be there just as revealed in God's Word.

Gold, as currently known, does not appear to be appropriate material for mansions and streets. Although gold does not tarnish nor rust, it is both the heaviest in weight and softest in texture of all of the gems mentioned in the portrait of heaven's construction. These liabilities would appear to make it a careless choice for either erecting rigid walls or suspending a lightweight floating city. However, don't expect to see grooves worn into the streets from constant strolling by heaven's inhabitants. Nor should one anticipate seeing the monumental city disappear from the radar screen due to excess weight. Neither of these mishaps will ever occur since the Master Creator will have completed his perfect plan in providing an eternal home for his own. Don't miss being in this group and spending eternity in this exquisite place!

Seldom is anything in life as rewarding as making a grand entrance. The wall around heaven will be equipped for regal admissions. The Holy City will be accessed by entering through one of 12 pearl gates. How could any entry be more elegant than passing through a gate made of a single large pearl, the queen of gems. Pearls are formed under the shells of water-dwelling creatures, mollusks. The beauty of them results from a reaction to an irritant. It is interesting that God selected pearls for gates. Would he, perhaps, be reminding the saints that he is aware of the numerous irritations and trials endured during our earthly sojourns? Perhaps he is saying to his saints, "You endured the tests, welcome home."

Using human logic, anyone suggesting that gates could consist of an oversized solitary pearl would be considered as drifting in dreamland. The largest pearl ever found was only three ounces in weight. This fact would hardly cause one to select these gems for providing 12 entry gates. But God said he'd have them placed strategically in heaven's walls and we may be assured it will be so.

The pearl gates will remain open at all times with an angel posted at each entry. Why do the gates remain open and why have an angel present? The exact answers to these questions have not been revealed; however, some interesting conjectures could be advanced. An open gate seems to signify a welcoming perspective. While Jesus lived on earth, he said all were welcome to enter God's Holy City. "For God so loved the world that He gave His only begotten Son, that whoever believes in Him should not perish but have everlasting life" (John 3:16). As a part of this welcome, he gave a prerequisite for entering heaven, namely, one must believe in Him. Leaving all gates to heaven open will be a reminder that Jesus saves sinful mankind and lovingly welcomes them into an eternal home.

The presence of an angel at each gate appears quite appropriate. No one or nothing failing to meet God's requirements will be allowed into heaven. Thus, a guarding angel provides a positive reminder that everyone is required to make a personal decision before being allowed passage through a gate into the New Jerusalem. All that transpires in the Holy City will be perfect and no sin or evil will ever be allowed to enter. Guarding against such wickedness will make heaven a highly desired eternal residence for God's redeemed children.

The names of the 12 tribes of Israel will be inscribed on the 12 pearl gates. Our gracious God included these names even though many of the Jewish people of his day, and those thereafter, ignored or rejected him. Surely, many from the gentile races have no better history, Christ has been rebuffed by masses of them also. All people can be joyful in knowing that Jesus was quite explicit when he said that heaven was prepared for, "whoever believes in Him." The inscribed pearl gates will be a reminder forever that God loves and accepts everyone; He holds no grudges.

What will the pearl gates contribute to the beauty of heaven? Their layered structure will cause them to radiate an iridescent brilliance. They are not transparent so light will not shine through them. However, they have an average refractive index and high double refraction capabilities so extraordinary displays of nearby colored lighting will be reflected from their surfaces.

What joy will overflow within the redeemed saints when they observe the magnificent view of the immense transparent golden Holy City, the huge gorgeous sparkling jasper wall, and the glory of the 12 large pearl gates. But there is much more! Massive displays of transmitted and reflected light rays will radiate from the gems within the wall. Imagine the fascinating thoughts that may be recalled as God's children reflect on the resplendent vista of this elegant wall. Perhaps some of the following images or applications may emerge.

Beautiful gems are universal and loved by most everyone throughout the world. As the saints view the numerous gems in heaven's wall, they will surely be reminded that God's love is universal, also. How could anyone, who was willing to sacrifice his only Son for the sins of mankind, ever escape eternal love and appreciation? That God sent Christ to die for those who were sinners and unworthy is humanly incomprehensible. If God displays such amazing love, how could anyone do less than tell others about his saving grace.

It is interesting to learn that, in addition to the identification of fool's gold, attempts have been made to duplicate many precious stones, thus producing and selling counterfeits or fakes. This is not unlike our world where Satan has numerous emissaries who are actually wolves appearing as sheep. They speak as children of God but have never really accepted his Son as the Lord of their lives. Likely, they have reasonable explanations for their fraudulent behaviors. It may be their need for public acceptance, respectability, or business advantage. These folks are everywhere, including numerous individuals who hold memberships in many churches. Christians must be careful to understand these impostors, but should always be ready to tell them about the promise of spending eternity in heaven through welcoming the loving Savior into their lives.

As gold is purified by intense heat so, too, are several gems improved in quality or color by heat, radiation, or other treatments. Special surface applications are occasionally used to correct blemishes or improve the appearance of gems. God often subjects his children to heated situations, special treatments, or difficult experiences. These trials are seldom enjoyable; however, when prayerfully reviewed, they generally allow the afflicted to see God's purposes through instruction, spiritual growth, or preparing one to comfort or meet the needs of others. Though possibly disheartened by life's difficult problems, it should be encouraging that God's ultimate purpose is to strengthen our lives and testimonies. As gems are enriched by harsh treatments so, too, Christians grow through adversities.

The gems of heaven vary from being transparent, translucent, to opaque. These attributes are not unlike the characteristics found in Christians. Many are thoroughly open and transparent regarding their faith and beliefs. These are generally those who are radiant and show courage in sharing their faith, making wonderful soul winners. Individuals who learn much about the Gospel and, thereafter instruct others, appear to have translucent qualities. They are often not bold up front witnesses; however, they are highly effective in teaching and sharing God's Word. Some of God's children appear to have opaque virtues, knowing much about God and his love and sharing this information with special people for specific needs. They appear fairly quiet and ineffective but these perceived traits are totally false. When folks are going through deep problems or grief, it's the opaque Christians who come to their aid. As found in gems, combinations of light emitting traits may also occur in Christians. They may have different mixtures of transparent, translucent, or opaque qualities, just as gems have varying light refractive and double refraction light indices. Similarly, Christians vary in the magnitude of their radiance, work, and energy. Some shine brightly at all times while others have bursts of energy. Whatever your qualities as one of God's gems, be available and active in exercising the wonderful gifts he has given you.

Great variations in costs and colors are found among gems. Some are highly expensive and rare, being treasured by only a limited number of wealthy owners or they are found in scattered museums throughout the world. Other gemstones are plentiful and lower in cost and may be enjoyed by numerous folks with lesser means. Regardless, the same color variants are often discovered in gems of differing qualities and prices. The all-knowing God has placed people of varying colors and economic strata together on His earth. Indeed, he has ably arranged for those from every race and economic level to serve as willing witnesses to all people, assuring that whosoever will may hear and come to His saving knowledge. God does not look on value or lineage as exceptional attributes but He expects faithfulness from all His children, regardless of their social status. Unfortunately, some museum-piece Christians, though enjoyable, never get out of their display cases to do much for Christ.

As already stated, some gems are available only in minimal quantities while others are present in great abundance nearly everywhere worldwide. God has his gems distributed in a similar manner. A few scattered Christians are very well-known, highly effective, and of tremendous value in relaying God's plan of salvation to mankind. They include exceptional Christian pastors, preachers, evangelists, teachers, and professors. Then there are the masses who appear to be of less prominence but are available worldwide to transmit the Good News of the Gospel. Certainly, these are not of reduced value to God, in fact, many of the lesser known individuals may earn even greater eventual heavenly rewards than the aforementioned renowned individuals. God certainly loves to use great talent but he needs and also loves anyone who is willing to serve.

Countless valuable health, protective, character, and intellectual enhancing benefits have been ascribed to gems over the centuries. Essentially all of these alleged benefits have been relegated to the realm of enjoyable humor. However, the day will surely come, when the redeemed view the gems in heaven, that thoughts about God's power and protection will surface. God alone has the ultimate might to heal the body and mind as well as give needed abilities and gifts to His children. Mankind has always had an innate desire for an indwelling power from somewhere to meet each need. Unfortunately, this power source, although always available, has often been ignored or denied. Most important, as we view the gems in heaven we'll be reminded again that God sent His precious Son, Jesus, to heal our sin-sick souls.

There are various grades of hardness among the different gemstones. Hardness of minds and hearts is no stranger to the Christian world. Some folks come to Christ easily but others resist for long periods due to hardness of their hearts. Mercifully, God doesn't quit, He wants the hard gems along with all the docile ones. Interestingly, the hardest gems accept the highest polish levels and can abrade precious stones that rub against them. Perhaps, some hard gems are necessary to bring other reluctant individuals to Christ; if so, they deserve to shine brightly.

Why are gems of different weights or densities distributed throughout heaven's foundations? Surely, modern day builders would place the heaviest gems in the lower foundations with the lighter stones at higher levels. God isn't going to do it our way; rather, He intersperses the heavy gems among those lighter in weight. Of course, does it really matter, the entire Holy City will be floating in space? Placement of the different weighted gems will be immaterial in ensuring the strength of heaven's wall. Perhaps, God's construction is designed to let frail humans know that He is able, not too worry!

While reading this book, it is obvious that the author allowed his thoughts to run freely regarding the actual musings that may occur among heaven's residents. Some or none of them my be correct; however, please consider heaven's gems carefully and draw your own conclusions. Certainly, whatever will be seen upon entering a pearl gate into the Holy City will be totally awesome. If you are not sure about your eventual destination, please read the next chapter. Hopefully, you will choose to spend eternity in heaven. Upon your arrival, let's explore heaven's wonders together!

Chapter 17
Heaven: A Decided Destination

Although described as a delightfully glorious eternal home, everyone talking, singing, reading, or thinking about heaven isn't going there. Sadly, there will be many who refuse to accept the requirements for entrance into this beautiful Holy City. Surely, the saddest aspect of missing eternal life in the Holy City would be spending forever in hell without God's care and the presence of His love. How dreadful it would be to spend eternity with the deceiver, Satan, who was never involved with anything that was good. Satan and the his lost followers will reside in a pit that will be devoid of divine illumination. Imagine dwelling with the presence of evil, torment and darkness throughout eternity.

The Good News is that our loving God has provided a wonderful alternative to residing forever in hell. If you, as a reader of this book about the splendor of heaven, are not absolutely assured that the Holy City will be your eventual eternal home, please consider the entrance requirements carefully. The Almighty God is the architect of heaven and, further, He sent his only beloved Son to earth to die on a cruel cross. His death paid the price for the sins of those who accept and receive Him as their personal Savior. Please do not ignore God's simple plan of salvation.

The Bible states clearly that we are all sinners. "For all have sinned and fall short of the glory of God" (Romans 3:23). Because of our sins, we are doomed to receive the punishment of death or separation from God. "For the wages of sin is death, but the gift of God is eternal life in Christ Jesus our Lord" (Romans 6:23). To dwell with God eternally, we must be made righteous in his sight. "For He made Him who knew no sin to be sin for us, that we might become the righteousness of God in Him" (2 Corinthians 5:21). God loves us even though we have sins in our lives. "For God so loved the world that He gave His only begotten Son, that whoever believes in Him should not perish but have everlasting life" (John 3:16).

One can come to Christ only through the free gift of grace, all the good things one does will fail to meet God's requirements for salvation. "For by grace you have been saved through faith, and that not of yourselves; it is the gift of God, not of works, lest anyone should boast" (Ephesians 2:8-9). By believing in Jesus, one receives eternal life. "These things I have written to you who believe in the name of the Son of God, that you may know that you have eternal life, and that you may continue to believe in the name of the Son of God" (1 John 5:13). God invites you to ask Jesus into your heart and life. "That if you confess with your mouth the Lord Jesus and believe in your heart that God has raised Him from the dead, you will be saved. For with the heart one believes unto righteousness, and with the mouth confession is made unto salvation" (Romans 10:9-10).

If you believe Jesus died for your sins, please pray the following prayer: *Jesus, I admit that I'm a sinner. I know you rose from the dead and I ask you to forgive my sins and be in control of my life. Right now, I accept you as my personal Savior. Thank you for saving my soul and for giving me eternal life. Help me to live for you daily and to be a witness for you. These things I pray in Jesus name. Amen.*

If you made this decision and prayed to accept Christ as your Savior, you are now one of God's redeemed children and are bound for an eventual life in heaven forever. Yes, heaven will be a magnificent and glorious eternal home. However, if one only knows about the beauty of heaven, this book will have failed to meet its intended purpose. God prepared this marvelous home for those who have accepted his Son as their Savior. Hopefully, you will share this message with all who need to know. My final remarks to you are, "I'll see you in heaven, WELCOME HOME!"

Selected Readings

1. Hall, Cally, *Gemstones*. Dorling Kindersley Handbooks, Inc., New York, NY. 2000.

2. LaHaye, Tim and Jenkins, Jerry, *Perhaps Today*. Tyndale House Publishers, Inc., Wheaton, IL. 2001.

3. Lucado, Max, *When Christ Comes*. Word Publishing, Nashville, TN. 1999.

4. Lutzer, Erwin, *One Minute After You Die*. Moody Press, Chicago, IL. 1997.

5. Post, Jeffrey, *The National Gem Collection*. Harry N. Abrams, Inc., New York, NY. 1997.

6.Schumann, Walter, *Gemstones of the World*. Sterling Publishing Co., Inc., New York, NY. 1997.

7.Schumann, Walter, *Handbook of Rocks, Minerals, & Gemstones*. Houghton Mifflin Company, New York, NY. 1993.

8. Walvoord, John, *Every Prophecy of the Bible*. Chariot Victor Publishing, Colorado Springs, CO. 1999.

Printed in the United States
65012LVS00014B/262-279